Acclaim for *Empire of the Son*

"Exquisite."
—Colin Thomas, *Georgia Straight*

"Understated perfection."
—Cecila Lu, *Vancity Buzz*

"Grief stripped raw in all its beauty."
—Erika Thorkelson, *Vancouver Sun*

"Gorgeous storytelling."
—Mark Robins, *Vancouver Presents*

"A profound piece of theatrical,
technical, and literary mastery."
—Olivia Law, *The Ubyssey*

Nominated for six Jessie Awards,
plus the *Georgia Straight*
Critics' Choice Innovation Award

EMPIRE
OF THE SON

TETSURO
SHIGEMATSU

Foreword by Donna Yamamoto
Introduction by Jerry Wasserman

Talonbooks

Talonbooks
278 East First Avenue, Vancouver, British Columbia, Canada V5T 1A6
www.talonbooks.com

Second printing: October 2017

Typeset in Arno
Printed and bound in Canada on 100% post-consumer recycled paper

Cover image by Ray Shum of Tempest Photography
Cover design concept by Terry Wong
Interior design by Typesmith
Interior photographs courtesy the author

Talonbooks acknowledges the financial support of the Canada Council for the Arts, the Government of Canada through the Canada Book Fund, and the Province of British Columbia through the British Columbia Arts Council and the Book Publishing Tax Credit.

Rights to produce *Empire of the Son*, in whole or in part, in any medium by any group, amateur or professional, are retained by the author. Interested persons are requested to apply to Tetsuro Shigematsu care of Talonbooks.

LIBRARY AND ARCHIVES CANADA CATALOGUING IN PUBLICATION

Shigematsu, Tetsuro, author
    Empire of the son / Tetsuro Shigematsu ; foreword by Donna Yamamoto ; introduction by Jerry Wasserman.

A play.
ISBN 978-1-77201-104-3 (PAPERBACK)

    I. Title.

PS8637.H522E47 2016   C812'.6   C2016-905951-0

In the end, I am not interested in that which I fully understand. The words I have written over the years are just a veneer. There are truths that lie beneath the surface of the words. Truths that rise up without warning like the humps of a sea monster, and then disappear. What performance in a song is to me, is finding a way to tempt the monster to the surface. To create a space where the creature can break through what is real and what is known to us. This shimmering space, where imagination and reality intersect, this is where all love, and tears, and joy, exist. This is the place ... this is where we live.

—NICK CAVE

Contents

When Everyone's Story Gets Told

Tetsuro and I joke it took an "arranged marriage" to bring us together. An occasional actor, Tetsuro auditioned to play my husband in Mortal Coil's production of *Salmon Row* by Nicola Harwood in 2011. This site-specific play, set in and around Britannia Heritage Shipyards at the mouth of the Fraser River in Steveston, relates the history of diverse communities of people who profited from the seemingly endless resource of salmon. Our show had a huge cast, but Tetsuro stood out for several reasons. He spoke so eloquently, and he could often be seen scribbling observations in his Moleskine notebook, plus he had a wicked sense of humour.

Cast friendships can be intense but are almost always short-lived. When *Salmon Row* came to an end, Tetsuro invited me to join the board of Vancouver Asian Canadian Theatre (VACT). I somehow had never attended any of their shows, though I knew this community theatre group was run by Joyce Lam, who was apparently looking for a successor. Tetsuro had just been elected president, so I went along. As an Asian woman who has been acting professionally since 1987, I understood the struggle. I know what it is like to be marginalized. Putting more Asians onstage? I'd vote for that, but little did I know that Tetsuro's first act in office would be to have me become artistic director. Joyce supported this idea, but I had absolutely no interest. I declined many times, but Tetsuro wouldn't take no for an answer. Finally I agreed. I sensed that a big change was coming. I had been acting for thirty years. TV was changing, film was changing, theatre remained a holdout. Now was the time.

When Joyce Lam graciously handed me the reins in August 2013, Tetsuro was pleased knowing that VACT's future had been secured. Perhaps because of that, I sensed he was losing interest in our organization. Maybe he thought his work here was done. One day I asked him over coffee in Chinatown, "What do you *really* want to do?" A little surprised by the question, he said he'd think about it.

In October 2013, around my kitchen table, what we were calling VACT 2.0 had its first annual strategic planning meeting with Tetsuro and a few core members, including Andrea Yu, Annie Jang, Belle Cheung, and Joyce Lam. I had given everyone a homework assignment: come up with two plays you would like to see VACT produce. We went around the table delivering our pitches, but when it came to Tetsuro, he hemmed and hawed, then mumbled he really didn't have anything. It was very unlike Tetsuro to blow off an assignment, so I teased him a bit before I began to move on to the next person. Suddenly, Tetsuro blurted that he wanted to do *his* show – he wanted to do his own one-man show. There were double takes all around.

Chances are Tetsuro will fade into oblivion like the rest of us, but if on the off chance that you do happen to know his name, then maybe you're thinking, "Yes of course, when Tetsuro Shigematsu volunteers to do a one-person show, you say yes!"

But keep in mind that back in 2013, Tetsuro wasn't Tetsuro Shigematsu – writer and performer of *Empire of the Son*. Back then, he was the only member of our company who had never been to theatre school. Sure, Tetsuro was a capable emcee for our annual general meetings and parties, but doing his own one-man show as our mainstage program? His proposition took us a little by surprise.

Did he have a script? No, but he had an idea. "I plan to discover vast worlds contained within my emotionally remote father. It will be a funny, emotional portrayal of parent-child relationships, and a reminder that no matter how far we journey out into the world to find ourselves – across decades and continents – we never stop being our parents' children." (Yes, believe it or not, Tetsuro really talks this way impromptu.)

Honestly, he had me at "father." As the daughter of a second-generation Japanese Canadian who is now eighty-nine years old and in his twilight years, I knew how rich and layered this story could be. I don't think I could ever tell my dad directly how much I love him, but through a great work of theatre, he just might be able to feel it. Plus everyone could relate to having a father. Perhaps sensing that not everyone was equally convinced as I was, Tetsuro stood up and said, "Why don't I just show you?" He channelled his father arguing with an adolescent version of himself. Soon everyone was smiling and nodding. We took a secret ballot and the results were unanimous.

Empire took countless hours to develop, including experiments in my basement using a live cinema camera and miniatures, readings at Historic Joy Kogawa House, performances at the Flame Storytelling Series, numerous workshops with wonderful creative artists and collaborators at the Roundhouse and the Firehall Theatre's B.C. Buds Spring Arts Festival, intensive sessions with director Richard Wolfe and dramaturg Heidi Taylor in Playwrights Theatre Centre's Test Kitchen, and many late-night grant writing sessions.

For two years, VACT bet everything on this one show. We were all in. Even though I supported him in every way, in the end it would be Tetsuro alone onstage. He alone would face the critics, his peers, his publics. As an untrained performer, he had the audacity to ask us for everything, and we were reckless enough to give it to him. If Tetsuro failed, there was no Plan B. VACT would close its doors. No pressure. When we would jokingly remind him of the stakes during board meetings, he would just shrug. For once, Tetsuro didn't have a witty comeback.

He was preoccupied with bigger pressures. His father's health was declining rapidly. To complicate matters further, Tetsuro had made a philosophical commitment to keeping *Empire of the Son* as factually accurate, real-to-life, and up-to-date as humanly possible. That may sound good in theory, but in reality it was wreaking havoc with his team of collaborators, who all required a final script to be nailed down. But there was simply too much drama happening in Tetsuro's family for him to stop making new additions to the text. When his father died just eighteen days before our run was scheduled to begin, his death left a giant crater in the work. They would have to change the beginning, the ending, everything would be affected. Tetsuro finally locked the script down several days prior to previewing. He had to. Because now he had lines to learn.

Then even before opening night, we began to feel the tremors. Something truly groundbreaking was beginning to happen. Before a single review had been written, *Empire of the Son* made history. To the best of our knowledge, for the world premiere of a Canadian play to completely sell out its entire run before opening, or even previewing, is unprecedented. Not only that, the holdover also immediately sold out.

Critics were unanimous in their praise. The *Vancouver Sun* named it the best show of 2015. The *Georgia Straight*'s Colin Thomas called it the most important show of the year. *Empire* went on to garner six Jessie nominations, including Outstanding Original Script, Outstanding Performance by an Actor in a Lead Role, Outstanding Production, plus the Critics' Choice Innovation Award (personally, I won the inaugural *Vancouver Now* Representation and Inclusion Award). From our humble beginnings in my kitchen, a growing national tour (so far the National Arts Centre in Ottawa, Centaur Theatre in Montreal, Factory Theatre in Toronto, Festival Players of Prince Edward County in Ontario, and Artistic Fraud of Newfoundland), the National Asian American Theater Association Festival in Ashland, Oregon, and this publication, I am still pinching myself in disbelief. But I have always believed in Tetsuro's talent. Tetsuro writes about things that matter to all of us with humour and a poetic grace that lifts the spirit. I am grateful to be a part of this adventure as his producer and friend.

I once observed a fellow theatre artist in the community congratulate Tetsuro on hitting a home run, but instead of simply accepting the compliment, he gave a little speech. "Sure I may have been the one holding the bat, but who surrounded me with a team of all-stars? Who got me into The Cultch, my Wrigley Field? Who made sure all the bases were loaded when I swung for the fences? It was Donna. Without her, this would have been a tiny show that no one ever saw except for family and friends. So who is the real MVP?" That was much more information than a simple compliment warranted, but I know Tetsuro feels strongly about this because I've heard him use this analogy several times.

Tetsuro's impulse to recognize the contribution of others is part of what makes him so easy to work with. In fact, I think many men might find it challenging to work for VACT because we have always been such a staunchly matriarchal organization. During VACT 2.0 all the leadership positions have been occupied by women. Even though Tetsuro has the longest history with the company, and despite being more than qualified, he has never displayed that male tendency to take charge.

One of the reasons Tetsuro works so well with us is that he doesn't take up all the conversation space, which is all the more remarkable considering he speaks for a living. But when Tetsuro does open his mouth, we pay attention because it's always clear he has been listening so closely. He'll sum up everything we have been talking about before offering his own thoughts.

By hanging back, he enables us to develop and flourish in our leadership positions, from Annie Jang, who joined VACT when she was just twenty-three years old, to me, who he personally persuaded to become artistic director. Even though I often introduce Tetsuro as my unofficial co-artistic director, he is always quick to interject, explaining he is simply my *consigliere*, a trusted advisor. And he is. Tetsuro shares his thoughts and opinions with me, but he always leaves the final decision to me. Even when he privately disagrees with my decisions, he publicly champions my choices with enthusiasm.

Even though our company has a cultural diversity mandate, and despite the fact that he publicly self-identifies as an artist of colour, I notice that whenever we hang out, Tetsuro tends to talk about gender even more than race: gendered roles, gendered labour, the gender order. Maybe it's because he has a daughter. Maybe it's because he was raised by the women in his family: his sisters and Yoshiko, his mom. In fact, if you have the chance to meet the women in his family, you'll see that each one is powerful in her own unique way, and they all stand in awe of the most powerful woman in his life, his partner Bahareh.

I believe it's all the women in his life who teach Tetsuro how to be a man, but maybe they go too far? Not only does he have long hair, but whenever I visit him at home he's usually wearing a skirt. But he also subverts gender norms in more meaningful ways.

One of Tetsuro's closest friends is a Tibetan artist named Kalsang Dawa, who didn't hesitate to express his disappointment in *Empire of the Son*. Kalsang had witnessed Tetsuro do incredibly witty impromptu performances. So after waiting to see what Tetsuro had been working on for two years, he said, "I just expected a lot more." Are your friends that honest? But there's a postscript to this story. Kalsang is a new father. His partner, Aranka, has just given birth to their second daughter, and he admitted to Tetsuro that even though he knows it's stupid, he couldn't help but feel a twinge of disappointment that she wasn't a boy. Kalsang is self-aware enough to recognize this as an outdated idea, but having grown up next to China all his life, he couldn't help but be influenced by a culture that prizes sons over daughters. Seeing Tetsuro onstage for less than seventy-five minutes was enough to change his mind. Kalsang confided in Tetsuro that now he realizes "having daughters is a *good* thing." This is the power of art. For all its bedazzling spectacle, its technical wizardry and all the powerful emotions it evokes, *Empire of the Son* is also a remarkably subtle piece of social criticism.

The other day, Tetsuro and I were driving to yet another meeting, and I saw this mural that read: "Never doubt that a small group of thoughtful, committed citizens can change the world; indeed, it's the only thing that ever has.—Margaret Mead." Tetsuro and I work unusually well together. I think it's because we can each do things the other can't, and yet we share the same values. We believe culture is more interesting when everyone's story gets told.

If you're thinking about changing the world, you can do it through art, but you can't do it alone. If you want to make a change in this world, you have to work across gender lines, across racial lines, across class. Open your eyes. Your potential allies are everywhere. Maybe even within the marriage someone else arranged for you.

—DONNA YAMAMOTO

The Terrible Beauty of Life

Tetsuro Shigematsu's *Empire of the Son* was the surprise hit of the 2015 Vancouver theatre season, selling out its run at the Vancouver East Cultural Centre and earning nominations for six Jessie Richardson awards. *Empire* surprised because it was almost entirely an unknown quantity: the first stage play in more than twenty years by a part-time playwright/actor best known for hosting a CBC Radio show that ended over a decade ago – performed solo by the playwright himself and produced by a low-profile (though rapidly emerging) local company.

It turned out to be a play of great emotional and theatrical intelligence: candid and funny, poetic and quietly moving. And this baby had legs. *Empire of the Son* was almost immediately booked for a 2016 remount at The Cultch, an Ottawa-Toronto-Montreal tour, and publication. These are no small triumphs for a new Canadian play by a little-known writer.

So meet Tetsuro. Born in England to Japanese parents; raised in Montreal and Vancouver with three sisters and a brother; a Concordia BFA in fine arts, UBC MFA in creative writing, and PhD candidate in education; husband to a Persian Canadian wife and father of two children. A sometime stand-up comic, visual artist, filmmaker, and a radio broadcaster like his late father, he thinks of himself as a contemporary inheritor of the samurai tradition; not just because, as a samurai descendant, he once fought a Viking on an episode of the MTV/Spike reality series *Deadliest Warrior* (2009–), but because, he says, the ideal samurai was not only a warrior but a polymath, versed in schools of philosophy and poetry as much as martial arts.

In *Empire of the Son*, a title resonant with intertext and pun, Tetsuro goes to war with the weapons of mind and heart, memory, technology, and some simple and profound theatrical poetry. He mostly battles himself, his own weaknesses. Facing his father's impending death, why couldn't he say "I love you"? And why, even now, can't he cry? A self-deprecating warrior, Tetsuro enlists the audience in this rehearsal for his father's funeral. He also looks to his family – mother and wife, and especially sisters and children – to help him make sense of his father's life and death, their father-son relationship, his own masculinity and identity, and mortality itself: what he calls near the play's exquisite conclusion, "the terrible beauty of life."

The central relationship in this play has echoes for me of English author Helen Macdonald's terrific non-theatrical memoir, *H Is for Hawk*, detailing her profound reaction to her father's death. It also made me think about fathers and sons in other plays like *Death of a Salesman*; David French's *Of the Fields, Lately*; Ins Choi's *Kim's Convenience*. But the training of hawks is not an issue here; nor is desperate failure or intense guilt. Intergenerational conflict is a minor theme and, though intercultural, *Empire of the Son* has no interest in identity politics. Those other plays filter biography and autobiography through fictitious characters and multiple actors whereas *Empire of the Son* is performed with the intense first-person immediacy of the auto/biographer himself in the room with us. Sometimes theatrically embodying his father (reminding me of a character played by Robert Lepage in his solo show *The Far Side of the Moon* transforming before our eyes into his dead mother), Tetsuro also employs recorded voices, photos and videos of family subjects, and props that are genuine relics of his father's life.

A fascinating character, Mr. Shigematsu (he hates being called Akira) is taciturn and emotionally unexpressive yet happy to share the bathtub with his children. Tetsuro's impressionistic portrait offers tantalizing glimpses of his father's ordinary/extraordinary life's rich subtexts, shadowed by the childhood firebombing of his Japanese hometown and the Hiroshima apocalypse. For Tetsuro, piecing together his father's biography serves more than just eulogy. It provides an ancestral mirror in which he sees himself reflected in a father-son continuum of four generations. Nursing his father through the terrible beauty of his final illness, Tetsuro achieves an awkward, embarrassing, and ultimately revelatory physical intimacy akin to what he has with his young son, Taizo.

Tetsuro's twenty-first century samurai sensibility also finds plenty of room to honour the women in his life. Although mother and wife get less stage time than father, they play central roles. Bahareh convinces Tetsuro to bring his parents to live with them, leading to a lovely moment when his mother exchanges her depressing isolation for a cacophony of grandchildren "more life-giving than springtime or birdsong." Tetsuro's daughter, Mika, becomes an important lens through which he sees his father's world. And if I had to choose a single scene to explain why I love this play, it would be the visit of Tetsuro's adult sisters, who lovingly pile onto his father's sickbed: "As I stand there, slack-jawed and dumb, in the corner of the room, all I can think is there are cultures in this world that prize sons more than daughters. I know because I come from one of them."

That kind of simple eloquence, a hallmark of the play, is also conjured by its vivid theatrical sleight of hand. Onstage, Tetsuro manipulates miniatures and a camera to create projected images of a ship at sea, a gliding ice skater, the Hiroshima mushroom cloud. Credit director Richard Wolfe and his design team together with Tetsuro for these compelling stage effects. A visual arts major in college and one-time feature film director (*Yellow Fellas,* which he also wrote, produced, edited, and starred in, released in 2007), Tetsuro describes himself as "utterly smitten by the power of the image." Theatrically, the device is magical. Thematically, it speaks to the creative capacity of the individual to remake the world and therefore him/herself.

Developed and produced by Vancouver Asian Canadian Theatre, *Empire of the Son* marks another small but significant step in the emergence of an exciting, diverse body of theatrical work from one of our country's most vibrant communities. From its roots in a typically complex Canadian nexus, a cross-roads of Japanese, Persian, and Canadian cultures, Tetsuro's story blossoms into an extraordinary paean to life itself.

—JERRY WASSERMAN

Silence an Ocean Wide

On the morning of October 23, 2015, at 10:23AM I received the following text from my friend Belle Cheung: "I think you should read this. I know her from school and she saw your show last night, sat in the first row." There below was a link to a Facebook post by someone I didn't know.

Social media is often decried for being a never-ending river of so much frivolous ephemera, but as a theatre artist I have come to see it as an alternative space – beyond the stage, beyond the lobby – where I can encounter my audience. Compared to the evanescence of sighs, laughter, compliments, embraces, or even bouquets, online remarks have the permanence of cuneiform clay tablets. I have never met Laura, but I have studied her off-the-cuff reflections as if they were the Rosetta stone, a clue to help me better understand an enduring mystery. In an increasingly mediated age, why do we keep coming back to this anachronistic form called theatre? What can happen in the space between the audience and performer that isn't possible anywhere else?

—TETSURO SHIGEMATSU

Okay, so thanks to Carolyn Nakagawa I got to see #EmpireoftheSon and was I the lone hipster girl softly weeping in the front row of one of the most intimate stages in Vancouver tonight? Yes, I was. And I got a little self-conscious that Tetsuro Shigematsu and I could have probably reached out and offered each other a Kleenex, but then I realized it was a play about crying and then I was the girl openly weeping in the front row aisle seat so absolutely everyone had to walk by me when the lights came up.

Maybe his words could have been my own? Maybe in my imagination, when he told the story of his father running from a burning Kagoshima, and then waiting at the train station looking for his own father after the war, I imagined my grandmother on that very same train several years later. I imagined what it must have been like to search for a home that had already burned, with no coordinates but the stories in her bones from her mother and father, like a salmon looking for a dry riverbed. I looked this man in the eyes and calculated the probability that our ancestors, Shigematsus and Suehiros, might have been friends.

I met a neighbour friend recently whose Japanese family immigrated to Vancouver in the early 20th century around the same time that my grandfather's family arrived, and I calculated the probability that her grandparents and my grandparents might have been friends.

There is a silence an ocean wide in how I *don't* identify as Japanese that I don't quite understand. I think I experienced something tonight that I catch glimpses of once in a while – like last week when Carolyn nonchalantly explained that "Yancha"means "Naughty mischievous imp" and my father has been calling me this all my life (I sort of knew it meant I was a brat).

Is this what cultural belonging feels like? Is it coincidence that a bomb and an ocean can blow us apart, and yet we still keep orbiting each other and finding these connections, almost by chance?

— **Laura Fukumoto**

Production History

The original production of *Empire of the Son* was produced by Vancouver Asian Canadian Theatre and presented by The Cultch, October 6 to 24, 2015. It was produced with the assistance of Playwrights Theatre Centre and developed at the 2014 PTC Writers' Colony in Vancouver. *Empire of the Son* was written in part with the support of the writer-in-residence program at Historic Joy Kogawa House.

WRITER AND PERFORMER	Tetsuro Shigematsu
ARTISTIC PRODUCER	Donna Yamamoto
DIRECTOR / ORIGINAL CONCEPT DRAMATURGY	Richard Wolfe
DRAMATURG	Heidi Taylor
SET DESIGN	Pam Johnson
LIGHTING DESIGN	Gerald King
COSTUME DESIGN	Barbara Clayden
SOUND DESIGN	Steve Charles
AUDIO DRAMATURG	Yvonne Gall
STAGE MANAGER	Susan Miyagishima
TECHNICAL DIRECTOR/ PRODUCTION MANAGER	Jayson McLean
PROPS MASTER	Carole Macdonald
VIDEO DESIGN CONSULTANT	Remy Siu
APPRENTICE STAGE MANAGER	Maria Zarillo
DOCUMENTARY AUDIO	Akira Shigematsu, Yoshiko Shigematsu, Rié Shigematsu Collett, Hana Shigematsu, Setsu Shigematsu
DOCUMENTARY VIDEO	Mika Shigematsu Taizo Shigematsu

Characters

All characters are played by TETSURO, with slight shifts of physicality and voice.

Family members (Mr. and Mrs. Shigematsu, AKIRA and YOSHIKO; Tetsuro's sisters, RIÉ, SETSU, and HANA; his brother, KEN: Tetsuro's wife, BAHAREH; their children, MIKA and TAIZO; and Bahareh's mother, MRS. POURGOL), are played by TETSURO.

Audio and video recordings of actual family members are seen and heard during the performance or appear as offstage voices.

EMPIRE
OF THE SON

(*above*) While standing with my back to the audience at the start of each performance, I take one last sustaining breath before diving in.

(*below*) A white tie for weddings, and a black tie for funerals. When my uncle in Japan shared this sartorial tradition with me, I was struck by the symmetrical symbolism of life and death.

A long table stage left is set with several small gooseneck lamps and groups of small objects. TETSURO operates a camera mounted on a slider dolly that rolls along the table, creating live video feeds that are projected on an upstage screen. Stage right, a chair, a small table with a drawer, and a microphone stand, with a brown leather briefcase on the floor. The drawer of the small table contains several objects to be used during the performance.

TETSURO walks onstage and stands with his back to the audience while stepping out of his traditional Japanese wooden geta clogs. Barefoot, he turns to the audience and bows. He remains barefoot throughout the performance.

In Japan, within the closet of any self-respecting Japanese man, you will find at least one black suit. And if you were to search the pockets of that suit, invariably you will find two ties, one in each pocket. A white tie, for all the weddings in his life. And a black tie, for all the funerals.

My father died on September 18. And I failed not once but twice. Two nights before he died, he was experiencing a rare moment of lucidity. So I asked him –

TETSURO: Hey Dad, how are you feeling?

AKIRA: *Ii kibun, ii kibun.*

"I feel good." And I had this impulse. You should say it! Now's your chance, just say it. It's only three words. But that's not something he ever said to me, so I wasn't sure how. So I said, "Good night, Dad." That night, he went to sleep and never woke up again. I didn't know that would be our last conversation. Two days later, he died. Our whole family was there. My sisters cried. I didn't. That was strike two. I feel like I have one more chance to get it right.

In Christianity, cremation tends to be frowned upon. But I think my parents may in fact be more Japanese than Christian because if you're Japanese, there's really only one cardinal sin – to be *meiwaku* – troublesome, a bother. So my father's instructions to us were to have his body donated to science. Which is great for us, because we save money. The thing is we won't get his ashes back for a while.

So now my father's funeral has been placed upon my timeline, and I'm watching it approach. And on that day, I'd like to be able to cry. I haven't cried since I was a kid. So I'm not gonna be able to just do it on the day of the funeral. Because if I do start to lose it, I'm gonna think oh wow, it's happening, I'm actually doing it. "Quick, someone take a photo! Instagram me!" – Ah, forget it, moment's passed.

For me to really cry at my father's funeral without self-consciousness, I figure I gotta cry at least a couple of times, so on that day, it'll be no big deal, just another emotion. So I want to thank you for coming out. Because this is not something I can do on my own. I just can't stand in front of the mirror at home and *will* myself to cry. Maybe that's something actors do. I don't know, I've never been to acting school. But I do have this "actorly" intuition. My sense is, if I open myself to you, and you open yourself to me, then maybe together we can summon a spirit I haven't felt since I was a kid. I have two kids, and they're gonna be there at my father's funeral. And when my kids see me being all friendly, shaking hands, making jokes, everyone else will be thinking, "Oh look at the good son, putting on such a brave front," but my kids will be thinking, Daddy really is a sociopath, superficially charming, but fundamentally lacking true empathy. Can't even cry at his own father's funeral.

So for me this capacity to cry isn't just a trivial matter, because I think the tenderness of our hearts is directly related to our capacity to feel joy. I mean, if there are no valleys within, can there really be mountain peaks? Maybe my interior is just a well-groomed golf course with slight undulations.

So tonight, we are going to explore geologically unstable territory. Together you and I will do a little jig over some fault lines and see what happens.

≈

The lights shift, and in shadow, TETSURO
pulls AKIRA's glasses out of the inner breast
pocket of his black suit and puts them on.
The lights come up, and he bows slightly.

AKIRA: (*with a Japanese accent*) My name is Shigematsu Akira. Please do not call me Akira. You may refer to me as Mr. Shigematsu. I take it some of you have paid money to listen to my long-haired son tell you stories. Please keep in mind they are just that. Stories. My son enjoys telling stories. Whenever someone asks me about my youngest child, I tell them: "My son makes fun of my accent for a living."

TETSURO: (*removing glasses to indicate he now plays himself*) Oh come on, Dad, do you really think this is a living? This is theatre! I took the bus here.

AKIRA: Need I say more? Imagine if you will, someone who thinks they know you so-o-o well, but in reality they do not understand you at all. Now imagine such a person has the temerity to perform a one-man show about you. Imagine what kind of purgatory that might be. *Irasshaimase!* Welcome to my world.

> *TETSURO places the glasses on the small table so that they face the audience. He produces a pair of yellow ear protectors from the leather briefcase.*

Exhibit A. These are the ear protectors my father, Akira Shigematsu, used at work.

> *He shows the ear protectors to members of the audience in the front row.*

He was not a construction worker. He did not operate a jackhammer. By the time he acquired these, he was on the verge of retirement, pushing a mail cart through the hallways of CBC Montreal. It was the last stop on a storied career as a public radio broadcaster. And these ear protectors were his attempt at social signaling.

> *TETSURO puts on the ear protectors.*

AKIRA: Don't talk to me. Stay away. I bite.

> *He removes the ear protectors.*

(*gesturing to their colour*) Hazard yellow.

This was my family's only heirloom, till last year when we received a telephone call from my Persian in-laws in Orange County. Now Farsi is a very courtly language. So my mother-in-law said, in the most flowery terms possible.

MRS. POURGOL: *Salam, Tetsuro-joon, bebakhshid,*
vali ma beh Newport Beach meeraveem, mifah-mi?

Translation? "We're moving to Newport Beach. Come get your
crap, or it's going in the landfill."

> *PROJECTION:*
> *STILL IMAGE of TETSURO and BAHAREH.*

That's my wife, Bahareh. Rhymes with *safari*. And together, we
move, a lot. All over the world. I don't know where I got such a
wanderlust, but it means we've accumulated a lot of stuff.

> *PROJECTION:*
> *STILL IMAGES of TETSURO and*
> *BAHAREH clearing out strange items.*

Mostly we ended up throwing everything away. But there were a
couple of things I just couldn't bear to part with.

> *PROJECTION:*
> *STILL IMAGE of a braid of hair.*

Not that, this.

> *TETSURO picks up the brown leather briefcase.*

This is my father's bag. When I was about nineteen years old,
I remember asking my dad if I could use it.

Sure, it was a request, but it was also kind of an offer. We had
been fighting a lot, and it was my way of saying, "Hey Dad, this
thing you own is actually pretty cool. And now that you no longer
appear to be needing it – why would a mail clerk need a briefcase
after all – how about passing it along. Father to son?"

My father refused, saying –

AKIRA: Only employees of the Canadian Broadcasting Corporation are legally entitled to use items emblazoned with the official logo of a Crown corporation!

TETSURO: Yeah right, Dad, somehow I don't think the police are gonna arrest me if they see me walking around with your stupid bag. What a loser.

He places the leather briefcase in
front of the small table.

For a long time, I did not like my father. I vowed to be nothing like him. I went to art school. Got involved with theatre. Started doing comedy, then one day a producer recorded one of my bits, then BOOM! I find myself working for CBC Radio. How does that even happen?

When I began hosting, management decided my voice didn't sound quite right. So they hired voice coaches who taught me to sound more *manly*. But apparently, I didn't sound manly enough, because they began trying out different microphones. At one point, they even had me speaking into a bass drum mic.

Opening the leather briefcase, he removes
a microphone case and then the mic.

Exhibit B.

The second object I managed to salvage from the landfill was this – (*holding up mic*). This is an Akai ACM-300 Electret Condenser microphone. This was my father's microphone. He was a public radio broadcaster.

I was a public radio broadcaster.

SOUND:
AUDIO CLIP of introduction in Japanese to
Akira Shigematsu's Radio Canada International
program, Canada Konogoro (Canada This Week).

TETSURO plugs in microphone on the mic stand.

Hi, I'm Tetsuro Shigematsu. You're listening to *The Roundup* here on CBC Radio One. Well you just met my father. Soon you'll meet the rest of my family, but first a bit of CanCon. This is Drake doing a cover of an Anne Murray classic –

SOUND:
AUDIO CLIP of Drake / Anne Murray mash-up.

≈

One of the cultural traditions my parents tried to keep alive in our household was bathing together. My mother explained to me that this was a way of preserving a vital part of our heritage. But I think it had just as much to do with the hot-water bill. When we were kids, my twin sister and I used to watch TV together before bedtime. And just when the show was getting really good, my mother would announce –

SOUND:
AUDIO CLIP of TETSURO's mother's voice.

MOM (*recorded*): Bath time!

We would wait until the last second before the commercial began, and then we would jump up, tear off our clothes, leap into the tub, wash our hair, wash each other, swim a few lengths, jump out, towel off, put on our pajamas, all within three minutes, back in time for the show to begin again. Cleanliness may be next to godliness, but we worshipped *Happy Days.*

(*above*) That's me with the belly hanging over the edge. Already, the body of a god; in my case, Buddha.

(*below*) When my kids came to see the show, they were not amused to discover that their missing toys had in fact been commandeered by Daddy.

PROJECTION:
STILL IMAGE of all the Shigematsu
children in the tub together, circa 1973.

Every so often my father would join us in the tub. And my twin sister and I would watch wide-eyed as the water level rose higher and higher, and just when we were sure that the entire house would flood, the water level would settle just below the rim, and we would holler, celebrating my father's Fuji-like mass. We took turns washing each other. My sister would shampoo my father's hair, and I would take a plastic cup and pour water down his back. My father was a mountain, a force of nature. He was my waterfall.

> *TETSURO goes to the long table and*
> *uses a glass to scoop water from a basin*
> *nested there. He pours water from the*
> *glass to create the effect of a waterfall.*

Back then, I thought everyone took baths together, until one day, third-grade gym class, this kid comes running up to us, all out of breath.

> KID: Hey you guys, I don't believe this myself, but
> somebody told me you two take baths together!
> That isn't true, is it?

My sister and I looked at each other, not knowing what to say. That night, we took our usual bath together, but we sat at either end of the tub and washed ourselves in silence.

> *PROJECTION:*
> *LIVE VIDEO FEED of TETSURO kneeling*
> *beside the long table and pushing the*
> *camera past a miniature bathroom set.*

≈

For me, these photos represent a time before, when Sundays were spent strolling along the River Thames, and a time after, when weekends were spent tooling around the junkyard.

PROJECTION:
STILL IMAGE of the Shigematsu
family in London, strolling along the
River Thames in the early 1970s.

This is my family before I was born. I don't know what you see, but when I look at my pre-me family, I see this perfect family leading this charmed life. I mean look at my brother. He's Harry Potter! I think even if you were a racist football hooligan strolling along the Thames and you passed my dad, I don't think you could help but say, "S'aright, for a Chinaman."

This is my father at his maximum portliness. Too much fish and chips maybe? When I look at my dad here, I wanna shout, "Enjoy the view, Dad! Soak it all in, because you'll never be happier than you are right now. Upon the fulcrum of old Big Ben there, your life is in perfect balance." But my mom, bless her heart, she is a woman of faith, and her faith was misplaced.

SOUND:
AUDIO CLIP of TETSURO's mother,
Yoshiko, talking with TETSURO.

MOM: (*recorded*) There was a rhythm method and there was maybe two or three days out of a month that when you DON'T get pregnant, and I was so sure. Dad thought about using precaution but, I thought oh, it's okay, because tonight is the two or three days I won't be able to – I won't be getting pregnant.

I then asked my mom, "How did you feel when you found out you were pregnant with me?"

MOM: (*recorded*) I wasn't uh … devastated.

Together, my twin sister Hana and I weighed less than one British stone, but that was enough to upset an otherwise perfectly balanced life. Congratulations on making it to the city of your dreams, Dad, but this won't be your final destination. Oh no, you're headed for the colonies. You fancy Savile Row, do you? How about Sally Ann? Today you are a voice on the BBC, but in your future I see yellow ear protectors.

When I used to look at family photo albums as a kid, the pictures I would always fixate on were of the backyard at 13 Red Post Hill in London.

> PROJECTION:
> STILL IMAGES of London home and backyard,
> with toddler TETSURO playing in a push car.

In particular I would always stare at the spectacular toys like the pedal cars, and I'd think how unfair that I used to ride them but I don't even remember. I'd ask my mom, "Do we still have that?" She'd laugh. I knew the answer was no, because I had asked before. But I guess I was hoping her answer might change.

≈

Not long ago an American senator was ridiculed for describing the Internet as a series of tubes, but in a way he was right. There are in fact transoceanic cables lining the ocean floor, carrying … everything. It's only in the last mile or so that the signals become airborne.

Much more ethereal is shortwave radio. Unlike AM or FM bands, whose signals fade in and out during road trips, shortwave radio has a global range. Its transmissions bounce off of particles in the ionosphere, before heading back down to earth.

When I was on FM radio, my voice would only extend as far as the next transmission tower, limited by the horizon, but my father's voice propagated around the world like a never-ending echo.

When we stand on the edge of a cliff famous for its echoing properties, how quickly we become at a loss for words after –

(*echoing through mic*) Hello! Echo! Can anyone hear me?

> SOUND:
> LIVE ECHO EFFECT *repeats*
> TETSURO's *question.*

A radio host has to be better than that. They have to keep on engaging you, drawing you in. They have to make smooth segues between unrelated ideas.

> *Lights up.*

One of the sadnesses of life is to feel the world move on without you.

My father spent a lifetime honing a set of skills only to see them become obsolete.

He used to cut his radio show together using a razor blade and tape, and now we have digital audio workstations.

In an age of GPS, what becomes of celestial navigation?

In an age of hookups, what happens to courting?

In an age of text messages, when was the last time you received a handwritten letter?

In an age of iTunes, do you even remember silence?

In an age of antidepressants, will you ever know the depths of despair?

When I was a kid, to me the sound of a distant train whistle was the saddest sound in the whole wide world. I had a pretty happy childhood, but for some reason, whenever I heard that sound, I would tear up. Tears would well up, roll down my temples, and fill my ears. There was so little melancholy in my childhood, it makes me wonder, where did such feelings come from?

≈

My dad took a long time to die. He had Parkinson's, Type 2 diabetes that left him completely blind, kidney failure, multiple strokes. When it became clear to us he didn't have a whole lot of time left, I took it upon myself to start recording his stories.

If you upload a recording of an interview to a digital audio editor, it'll look like a mountain range.

>*PROJECTION:*
>*VIDEO of waveforms.*

But conversations with my father don't look like that. Our conversations look like Canada. Between my questions, which are the Rockies, and his answers are these long prairies of silence.

>*PROJECTION:*
>*VIDEO of waveform moving in*
>*time with an audio recording.*

>*SOUND:*
>*AUDIO CLIP of TETSURO interviewing AKIRA.*

TETSURO: (*recorded*) Did anyone in your family go to war?

A long flat line represents silence.

AKIRA: (*recorded*) Yeah, my father went to the war.

>*AUDIO OUT.*

~

Years ago, I found a photo which I have since lost. But it's okay because I can still see it. It's this sepia-toned shot of a handsome young Asian man standing on a beach. He is very well-dressed. He has on a white linen shirt, khaki trousers. On the back of the photo it reads "Dad and Hugh, Isle of Wight." – Hugh is my middle name – I was born in London. And in this photograph, I am barely visible, a small infant fast asleep in his arms.

And I'm amazed that I could've ever been so small to have been held, and that he could've ever been so large to hold me.

I like to think my father is looking out across the Atlantic, trying to imagine what life was going to be like for his young family in Canada.

≈

My dad began writing his memoir. He didn't get very far. Just one page. But I have it.

> TETSURO *opens the drawer of the small table, picks up a page, and reads.*

"My name is Shigematsu Akira, and I am from Japan but my story begins here in England. I had brought my wife and children from Japan to live here in London. For the past five years, I had been working for the BBC as an announcer/producer for external services. But now my contract was up."

> TETSURO *continues in character as AKIRA, as the father takes over telling his story.*

AKIRA: One day I was walking around the corner of Trafalgar Square when I came across the small offices of Thomas Cooke. The front glass had three large posters.

One was a palm tree tilting over the white crest of a gentle wave.

The middle one was an enticing picture of Australia by Qantas Air.

The one on the right was a bird's-eye view of a white ship cruising through an azure ocean.

I walked into the office.

17

A middle-aged man was at the counter. I asked, "Is there any boat that goes to Canada?"

"Yes," he said, "there is one departing next January, one cruise ship of P&O is sailing from Southampton and is calling Vancouver."

I thought to myself, January is a perfect time. By that time I will be jobless and free to go anywhere.

I had already applied for us to emigrate to Canada. But I do not know what the result will be.

Even if it fails, my family and I can still go there as tourists. Then we can choose Japan as our last destination.

In this age of jet planes, it would be a bit of fun to travel by the ancient method of seafaring.

> PROJECTION:
> LIVE VIDEO FEED of TETSURO placing a small paper boat in a tub of blue water nestled in the long table. Using a drinking straw, he gently blows to move the boat across the water.

> PROJECTION:
> VIDEO of paper boat as it is blown across the tub and out of view.

≈

> SOUND:
> AUDIO CLIP of loud 1980s speed metal.

*TETSURO moves the camera down the
table, and leaps to his feet propelled by
the energy of the thrashing guitar.*

It's the 1980s, and I'm a teenager! My family is living in
the leafy suburbs of Montreal, in a most un-radical 'hood
called Pointe-Claire.

Ideologically, as a teenager, I self-describe as an anarchist, and I'm
about to express that ideology with my skateboard – when my
father steps into the driveway, totally cramping my style.

*PROJECTION:
LIVE VIDEO FEED of TETSURO's two
fingers powersliding into the frame on top of a
miniature skateboard, immediately joined by
a second pair of fingers. The fingers represent
the legs of TETSURO and AKIRA.*

AKIRA: Where do you think you're going?

TETSURO: Skateboarding. You got a problem with that?

AKIRA: Yes, problem. You skateboard too much! That is
problem. Go pull out weeds in vegetable garden!

TETSURO: Aw Dad, can't we get a gardener for that?

AKIRA: Gardener?! When I was your age, we had no
garden, no house. Everything was destroyed.

TETSURO: Well duh! Isn't that why you like left Japan? So
we could have a better life? Well this is it, Dad. This is it!

Now if you'll excuse me there's a new flavour of Slurpee
down at the 7-Eleven I need to go try, so if we're done here,
domo arigato, Mr. Roboto.

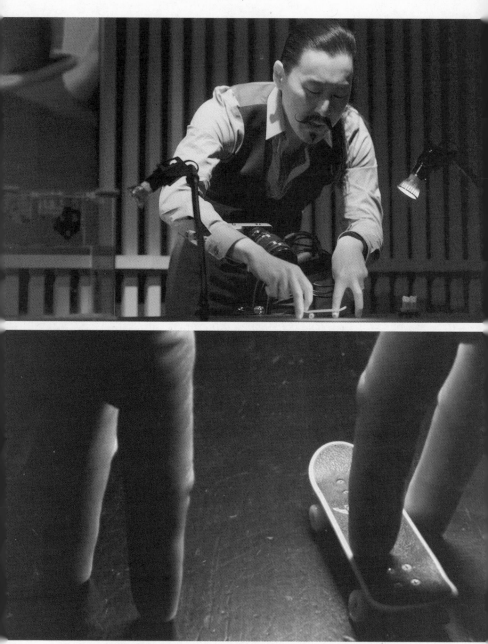

According to my director, Richard Wolfe, apparently I have unusually expressive fingers. Two thumbs up!

And with that he grabbed my skateboard and hurled it across the driveway.

> *TETSURO flicks the skateboard into his hand.*
> *VIDEO OUT.*

My father and I have a tempestuous relationship. I mouth off, and we go a couple of rounds.

He rarely speaks at the dinner table so when he does it's something of an occasion. Usually he's plugged into his shortwave Walkman listening to news reports from the BBC or Japan.

So when he began removing his earbuds, all heads turned to pay attention.

> AKIRA: Tetsuro, I have been thinking about this idea for some time now, in fact just over a year, and I think the time is approaching for me to share it with you.

And with that he replaces his earbuds, and resumes eating.

My twin sister Hana begins taunting me, "Ha, ha, you're in trouble!"

It turns out my dad just wanted to go for a drive.

> TETSURO: And where would you like to go for a drive, Dad?

> AKIRA: I was thinking perhaps Boston. I hear the trees are lovely in New England this time of year.

We never got to Boston. We stopped at a motel on the outskirts of the city. A cheap motel. The kind that would likely offer you a discount if you only needed it for a couple of hours.

My father comes out of the bathroom, hair neatly combed, shirt tucked in. He's ready.

He sits down on the edge of the bed. It's a strange intimacy to share a motel room with your father.

Apropos of nothing, he begins.

> AKIRA: If I could change one thing about my life, it would have to be the fact that as a child, I never played intramural sports.

> TETSURO: We drove all the way down to Boston so we could talk about your memories of gym class?

> AKIRA: As I was growing up, I never engaged in many social activities. I see this pattern repeating itself in your life. I do not want you to become what I have become, a social hermit.

> The Chinese have a saying: may you live in interesting times. In my life, I have lived in interesting times. In your life, you have lived in the suburbs. The suburbs may produce a Mendelssohn, but they cannot produce a Beethoven. The way I see it, you can go to one of three places: Calcutta, the Bronx, or Winnipeg.

> TETSURO: Calcutta, India?

> AKIRA: Yes, I want you to work among the lepers with Mother Teresa.

> TETSURO: What about Winnipeg?

> AKIRA: Ah yes, Mother Teresa has a mission there also.

I found the idea ludicrous and yet strangely appealing. The narcissistic side of me saw India as a backdrop for an epic story in which I would play the main character. Tetsuro of Arabia.

> TETSURO: And when would you have me go?

AKIRA: As soon as we get back.

TETSURO: But Dad, you can't afford to send me to India.

AKIRA: Don't worry about the money. That is none of your business!

TETSURO: Fine. What about school?

AKIRA: This will be your education.

TETSURO: But Dad, I've already registered. I'm going into my second year.

AKIRA: Get a refund!

It was the classic parent-child argument but someone had switched the lines. I tried to explain to my Asian father the value of a university education.

AKIRA: Nonsense, you must find yourself.

Back in Montreal, my twin sister Hana asked me –

HANA: Is it true? Are you seriously going to India?

And I remember saying, kind of loudly, "India? Why would I want to go there?"

We fought again. It was bad. No punches were thrown, but we hurt each other in other ways.

In the end my father wrote me this handwritten letter.

> TETSURO *produces a letter from the drawer.*

> PROJECTION:
> STILL IMAGE *of handwritten letter.*
> *He begins to read the letter.*

January 4, '93

Dear Hugh,

> *SOUND:*
> *AUDIO CLIP of AKIRA (performed by*
> *TETSURO) reading his letter.*

AKIRA: (*recorded*) I was wrong in trying to impose a fancy idea upon you. I withdraw my proposal. You don't have to contact the Missionaries of Charity. Your trip to India with your parental support is now off. Enjoy summer as you like.

Respectfully, Dad

> *He puts the letter down. Projection out. Lights out.*

≈

> *TETSURO stands at the small table.*
> *He picks up AKIRA's eyeglasses and*
> *studies them, lost in thought.*

When people tell stories of how they witnessed something important, a brush with death, meeting someone famous, we have this tendency to place ourselves closer and closer to the centre of the action with each retelling.

My father is not like that. He keeps himself on the periphery, which would be fine if it weren't for the fact that, to me, my dad is Forrest Gump, the Zelig of the twentieth century.

For example, did you know my father had tea with the Queen of England? It's true! But to hear him tell it, all he'll say is –

AKIRA: I was not the only one there.

When pressed, the most he'll concede is –

AKIRA: Prince Philip had a very dark tan. Perhaps he had been spending too much time playing polo while the rest of his British subjects toiled indoors.

That's it. End of story. Talk about a waste of an invite.

Did you know my father was there when Marilyn Monroe sang "Happy Birthday" to JFK? It's true. But to hear him tell it, all he'll say is –

AKIRA: I was not the only one there.

When pressed, the most he'll concede is –

AKIRA: Ms. Monroe appeared to be a very passionate woman, perhaps even in love with the president. But how could I enjoy the proceedings when Mrs. Kennedy was sitting right beside him? For me the whole evening felt very awkward.

So I feel like these brushes with history are wasted upon my father. And none more so than August 6, 1945.

SOUND:
AUDIO CLIP of CBC Radio interview
between AKIRA and TETSURO. The piece
aired with Stephen Quinn, guest-hosting
for Kathryn Gretsinger on The Afternoon
Show, CBC Radio One, August 6, 2003
(anniversary of the bombing of Hiroshima).

AKIRA: (recorded) Are you checking about my degree of Alzheimer's?

TETSURO: (recorded) He doesn't really have Alzheimer's, just a dark sense of humour.

AKIRA (recorded): August the ... Oh! August the six. That's a, that's a ... Hiroshima was attacked. I was twelve years old. It was just like today's in terms of the brightness

Stage manager Susan Miyagashima spent long nights testing ways to create the impression of a mushroom cloud until she discovered cream injected into water. BOOM!

of sky. It was a very bright August day. The city was flattened, that's all, just darkness, and there was no electricity. And no sign of civilization. I had some physical ailment after the passing of Hiroshima station. I don't know whether it was the effect of atomic radiation or not, but probably not. Probably it was due to some food poisoning.

> PROJECTION:
> LIVE VIDEO FEED of TETSURO taking a large syringe filled with cream and injecting it into an aquarium filled with water to create a ghostly mushroom cloud.

> PROJECTION:
> STILL IMAGES of a miniature ruined city fill the projection screen.

> VIDEO OUT. AUDIO OUT.

≈

Interviewing my dad. I'm a pretty good son, don't you think? I'm a pretty good father. In fact, I'm just a pretty good, all around human being. Complete. Fully evolved. Or so I thought, until –

> PROJECTION:
> VIDEO of TAIZO and MIKA, TETSURO's kids, eating pizza with TETSURO behind the camera.

TETSURO: (recorded) What do you want to talk about?

TAIZO: Have you ever cried a real cry in your life?

TETSURO: Yeah, of course.

TAIZO: Like a real cry.

TETSURO: Yes.

MIKA: When you were a grown-up?

TAIZO: Yeah, when you were a grown-up?

TETSURO: Oh, uhm. I probably have.

TAIZO: 'Cause I never seen you cry before.

TETSURO: What do you think, Mika?

MIKA: That'd be unusual. You have never crone before in your life.

TETSURO: Why do you think I don't cry?

MIKA: You're like strong like you don't get hurt easily and cry that's what I mean.

TETSURO: But strong people cry. Crying is a sign of strength.

MIKA: Then you're not that strong because you've never crone when you're a grown-up.

TETSURO: I guess so.

VIDEO OUT.

I never gave my kids an answer that day. How come I never cry? I guess the short answer is, I never cry because my father never cried, and he never cried, because his father never cried, and so on, and so on. So it makes me wonder, within my ancestry, who was that original idiot who stopped crying and ruined it for the rest of us? And who is gonna break that chain?

PROJECTION:
STILL IMAGES of TAIZO crying.

(*with admiration*) My son Taizo appears to be going for it. He's eight years old, and he'll cry with very little prompting.

(*as TAIZO, crying*) There's pulp in my orange juice. I don't like pulp in my orange juice!

That's not fair. Because the one thing I really do admire about my son Taizo is that he isn't afraid to express his emotional needs. Let's say he's feeling all alone. The kind of existential loneliness only a child can feel after having been all by himself on the toilet for a full ten minutes, which in child years must seem like forever, so Taizo will yell out, "I don't want any privacy!" Which is his way of saying "I'm lonely." And when I walk into the bathroom, he'll look up at me and say –

TAIZO: Daddy, will you wipe my buttinsky?

Yes, it's my job to wipe my boy's butt. He loves it! For him, it's like a day at the spa. He'll loll around, and we'll have conversations, like –

TAIZO: Daddy, can I keep this toilet roll?

TETSURO: Sure?

TAIZO: Good, because I wanna use it as a telescope.

> *TETSURO holds the toilet roll to
> his own eye. Looks at members of the
> audience, then up at the moon.*

≈

We look at the moon so often, but what does the moon see when it looks down at us? All that time, staring, unblinking. Probably not much. Over four and a half billion years? The drift of continents? Even from a lunar perspective, that's gotta be boring.

I figure there were two events that would have made the moon go, "Huh. Something's going on down there." According to my son, a gigantic asteroid destroyed the dinosaurs and almost everything else here on earth sixty-five million years ago. And then ...

August 6, 1945, Hiroshima, arguably the epicentre of human history. The one moment in time that changes everything. My father glimpsed the end of the world, but to hear him tell it, it was an episode of food poisoning. So my father isn't the best storyteller, I mean, he has a good memory, but he lacks imagination.

My daughter Mika is twelve years old. The same age my father was when he was in Hiroshima. And for me, Hiroshima does not hit home, until I imagine my daughter, all sixty pounds of her, riding alone in a boxcar during the closing months of yet another world war, just trying to get to another place that might be safer. And when her boxcar stops somewhere in the middle of the night, she sees the aftermath of a new weapon so terrible it destroys all meaning. An experience so traumatizing she can't share it with her own children.

My daughter Mika is like me. She doesn't lack imagination. In fact, sometimes she'll become sad for no apparent reason.

Once I came to her at night because she was weeping softly in bed. "What's the matter?" She was thinking about our family ice skating on Grouse Mountain one last time, before the sun came up. Her answer disturbed me because she was reliving something that never even happened. You see she had written this story for school.

> SOUND:
> AUDIO CLIP of MIKA reading her story.

MIKA: (recorded)

The Brightest Moon by Mika Shigematsu

One night after I finished my homework my mom told me to come out and look at the moon. I thought that was weird because my mom claims I don't get enough sleep. People were crowding outside on the street with their radios. So we decided to get ours too. We turned it on. We heard that the other side of the earth was being scorched by a giant solar flare. That's why everybody was outside in the middle of the night. By sunrise we would be dead. We decided to spend the rest of the night skating on Grouse Mountain one last time. Once we got there, we skated for a bit, until the sun peaked over the mountains. That was the prettiest thing I ever ... (*her voice breaks*)

> *AUDIO OUT.*
> *Lighting changes. Music up.*
>
> *PROJECTION:*
> *LIVE VIDEO FEED OF TETSURO's*
> *fingers gliding between banks of sugar like an*
> *ice skater at a snow-edged skating pond.*

Is the imagination so powerful that it can conjure stories so haunting that they can scarcely be retold? Or maybe my daughter is somehow reliving my father's trauma, a story she's never even heard, yet somehow still echoes inside her.

For my son, the saddest thing in the whole wide world is the extinction of the dinosaurs, and I think the moon might agree. An asteroid colliding with our blue planet must be a terrible thing to witness. But right up there, from a lunar perspective at least, would be the flash of a weapon so bright, so bright it blinds the moon.

≈

January 22, 2015. I'm with my father in the hospital, interviewing him about his hometown of Kagoshima. He had never been so candid. I'd love to play it for you, but I've lost the tape. I find it uncanny that the one piece of audio which captures him completely unguarded is gone. It's almost as if my father willed it out of existence. But I know it happened, because I have the transcript.

TETSURO gets the transcript from the drawer of the small table and begins reading through a microphone for AKIRA's voice.

AKIRA: On the night of June 17, 1945, in Kagoshima, I was awakened by a bright light nearby our house. It was an incendiary raid. They came in waves. Incendiary is particularly effective for Japanese town which is made of wood and paper. I remember the sound of houses burning down. It is like a huge bonfire. It is getting hot.

We took shelter outside the house, just a few yards away. Because the neighbouring houses were on fire, it was inevitable our house would be engulfed by the great fire. Then Mama said, Let's get out. I remember walking and running. The sky was red. It was midnight. I am always grateful for my mother's decision, otherwise we would have burned alive inside the shelter.

TETSURO: Where did you go?

AKIRA: All the public shelters were flooded from the heavy rains. I remember the families in the streets. The single parents cannot take care of all of their children, so a mother or father would try to give their child away. They asked passersby to take care of some of their children. They just take no responsibility for the safety of their neighbour's children. That's how some of the children lost their lives.

TETSURO: How long did the fire last?

AKIRA: Maybe twenty-four hours or more. The next morning the asphalt was still hot beneath our feet. My last memory of my house – was still intact – but a few hours later it was completely burned down. That was the end of the world.

TETSURO returns the paper to the drawer, pausing for a moment.

≈

SOUND:
AUDIO CLIP of loud workout music.

TETSURO leaps to his feet and shadowboxes.

I work out. Obviously. Maybe you think I'm vain. You have no idea. I am deeply shallow. This is how shallow I can be. When I shop, I only look for short-sleeved shirts. I don't even bother trying them on. This is what I'll do. I'll slip my arm into the sleeve from the outside and if it's baggy then forget it, but if it's snug, if it starts getting really tight at the top of my flex, it is on! We are taking a trip to the cash register.

Working out is a pretty recent development for me. So I don't know what the rest of you think about when you work out. But me, I think about my dad.

He would fall down and have to go to the hospital. So that leaves me a lot of time alone with my father. Now I don't know if you've ever done a bedside vigil, but a strange thing happens to time about five or six hours in, it's as if the second hand of the clock goes tick tick ... tick.

Now I'm no foodie. Maybe I'll bring in a meal of dry chicken breast over some brown rice, stick it in the fridge. But I'll start thinking about that meal like it's a lover calling to me. I'm not even hungry, but I'll find myself longing for this meal. When time becomes interminable, you start looking forward to the smallest things.

I'll be in the middle of one of these reveries when my father will wake up and say "B.M." Times like this, there is no time to page a nurse. Stand up. Clear a path. Lower the bed rail. Swing his feet over. Put my hands beneath his armpits and lift.

> *TETSURO's arms rise as if they*
> *were tied to helium balloons.*

I feel like I could carry him with one hand. He's never been so light. I've never been so strong.

We're in a tiny hospital bathroom. I lift up his blue gown, pull down his diaper, and my father keeps saying "I'm sorry, I'm sorry." And I want to say, "You got nothing to be sorry about, Dad. I got this. I can carry you. I can carry Mom. I can carry my kids. I could put all of you on my back and crush ten reps." But that's not what I say. I'm not here. I'm in a tiny hospital bathroom. And my father keeps saying "I'm sorry, I'm sorry" and I don't know what to say.

≈

> *SOUND:*
> *AUDIO CLIP of TETSURO's mother*
> *reading* Momotaro *in Japanese.*

When my twin sister and I were four years old, my mother was reading us a story before bedtime, *Momotaro* – a Japanese storybook, which we could kind of understand, but not completely. "English, read it to us in English."

And I remember the look on my mother's face. She was tired. We were being whiny.

> *TETSURO becomes his mother*
> *reading* Momotaro.

> MOM: Once upon a time, there was an old couple, who did not have any children ...

That was the last time my mom ever read to us in Japanese.

≈

The one time I remember being really impressed with my dad was when he brought home two grocery bags, not the plastic kind you get today, but two big brown paper bags – like gigantic lunch bags – and they were full of mail. Fan mail. Handwritten letters, maps of hometowns. Hockey magazines in Japanese! But mostly I remember the portraits, selfies really. Men in Japan of all ages would enclose photos of themselves posing next to their shortwave radio setups. These were the *otaku*, highly intelligent, but socially inept ultra-geeks, and my father was their king.

There is a part of the Japanese brain that has a special affinity for the idea of Canada. If you're a salaryman in Japan, leading a life of quiet desperation, riding crowded subways, sleeping in capsule motels – the wide open spaces of *this* country, with its dude ranches, its leaping salmon, its noble moose – all this holds special appeal. Canada is the anti-Japan. Unlike his legion of listeners, my father managed to leave planet Tokyo. He achieved escape velocity during a time when its gravitational pull should have been at its very strongest.

≈

It's the mid-nineties, and I'm teaching English in Tokyo. Evening rush hour. I'm wearing my navy blue suit, briefcase in hand. I'm admiring my reflection in the window, when I realize it's not me. From all the other salarymen, I can't pick myself out. We all have the same hair, same clothes, same posture. And for a moment, it's easy for me to imagine that I'm not just looking into a mirror, but through a window into the past.

PROJECTION:
LIVE VIDEO FEED of a miniature Tokyo
subway train glued to the display of an iPhone
that plays a video of the passing cityscape.

I can see my father riding this same train. He's a young Keio University graduate in Tokyo during the post-war economic miracle. He's the right age, at the right place, at the right time. "Why did you leave, Dad?" The train lurches. I look around and see what he must have seen. People with the same hair, same clothes, same posture. Is it me, or is there not enough air in this car?

Video out. Lights up.

≈

It's my father's back I remember most.

In our home in Surrey, B.C., his desk consisted of a red door resting on a pair of cinder blocks. On top of it sat this big reel-to-reel tape recorder where he'd take his raw tape and splice together his radio program. As a kid, I would sit in the hallway just outside his office and play with his shortwave radio. It had this giant knob on the front, and when I turned it, it was like I was turning the world.

*PROJECTION:
VIDEO of a mandala of radio waves
expanding endlessly on the projection
screen and beyond to the entire wall.*

*TETSURO speaks quietly into the microphone,
but his voice fills the space as if he were whispering
directly into the ears of the audience.*

Between clouds of static, I could tune into more languages than I knew existed. The tappings of Morse code, the chatter of amateur radio operators, fishermen sending out SOS on storm-tossed seas.

It was like closing your eyes and swimming through the world's fevered dreams.

But it was between the signals where I lingered. Because there in the static I could hear barely human, sentient entities. Their moaning, plaintive cries terrified me and yet I couldn't pull away. I thought I had stumbled into purgatory somehow. These were the souls doomed to wander the netherworld, blindly careening off the ionosphere, completely oblivious to a little kid tuning into their suffering via shortwave radio.

≈

I've been Googling my father's radio program for years now, but nothing ever came up. Turns out I was spelling it wrong. It's not *Canada Kono Goro, Canada These Days*. It's *Canada no Wadai, Current Topics on Canada*. Duh! When put in quotation marks, Googling *"Canada no Wadai"* yields one result –

> *PROJECTION:*
> *STILL IMAGE of a radio show episode list.*

This is a PDF hosted by the library of the University of British Columbia. Jackpot. This document is an inventory of the Radio Canada International Recordings Collection, which is where I found this –

> *TETSURO goes to the leather briefcase and produces a vinyl record of his father's recording.*
>
> *SOUND:*
> *AUDIO CLIP of segment from Radio Canada International's Canada no Wadai (Japanese Topical Discs, JTD 90, Radio Canada International Recordings Collection, 1977–1987, University of British Columbia Archives). AKIRA's voice in Japanese.*

My father began broadcasting with the BBC before I was born.

And he only stopped when Mulroney shut down RCI's transmitter twenty years later.

Two decades' worth of programming is a lot of shows, but I never listened to a single minute until a full quarter century after he stopped broadcasting. I'm not proud of this, but it has been theorized that echoes never disappear completely.

For my father, some echoes never stopped. In the middle of the night, he would yell out in his sleep –

AKIRA: Don't call me Akira!

At the end of his career, due to cutbacks, my father was demoted, from voicing and producing a radio program with the second-highest ratings in its category worldwide, to pushing a mail cart.

For my dad the biggest loss was having to leave behind the silence of the recording booth. Because now he was subjected to the casual intimacy of hearing his given name again and again.

> TETSURO speaks through a handheld
> mic with an echo effect.

> SOUND:
> LIVE ECHO EFFECT intensifies TETSURO's
> impression of CBC Radio employees'
> playful attempts to banter with AKIRA.

AKIRA's CO-WORKERS: (echoing through mic) Depeche-toi, Monsieur Akira! Ça va bien, Akira? Comment allez-vous, Akira! Akira, Akira, Akira.

It was too much. He couldn't just flip a switch or pull a fader, so in the end, he attenuated the signal.

> TETSURO puts on the ear protectors.

PROJECTION:
LIVE VIDEO FEED of TETSURO walking
his fingers slowly across the camera's frame,
then pulling a miniature red wagon that
carries two brown paper bags full of mail.

≈

Every time my father went into the hospital, it seemed less and less likely that he would ever come out. Conference call with my sisters. "How is Dad doing? Should we come?" And I stopped.

My sisters never ask my advice about anything. I'm the baby of the family. But here they were. "Tetsuro, tell us. Should we come?" If they don't come and something happens, I'll never live it down. But for some reason I can't bring myself to say it. So I say, "Listen closely because I'm only going to say this once. No one here is telling you *not* to come."

My sisters booked their flights from all points to Vancouver, indirect flights, weird connections, and by some coincidence all three sisters landed at YVR within thirty minutes of each other. As we all piled into my car, everyone was giddy, literally giggling. Sure the circumstances were crappy, but this was an impromptu family reunion. We only saw each other once a year, if that. But now we were all together, and everyone was so happy.

PROJECTION:
STILL IMAGE of TETSURO's sisters, HANA,
RIÉ, and SETSU, and TETSURO in the car.

As I began driving towards St. Paul's, one of my sisters said –

SOUND:
AUDIO CLIP of HANA, RIÉ, and
SETSU talking with TETSURO in the
car on the way to the hospital.

(*above*) In matters of intervention, it is the prerogative of the twin sister to disregard personal boundaries.

(*below*) Dad was so dehydrated he needed to be hospitalized. My sisters noticed he was lethargic. My brother and I did not.

HANA: (*recorded*) By the way, we are not really here for Dad. That was just a pretext.

RIÉ: The real reason we're here is because we decided it was time to stage an intervention on your moustache.

SETSU: We're serious, it's over the top. We think your facial hair is extremely aggressive, and aggressively antisocial. It's really going to limit your opportunities.

HANA / SETSU / RIÉ: Yeah, you look really untrustworthy / dubious / supercilious / insouciant / oleaginous.

Did I mention my sisters all scored within the top one percentile on their SATs?

(*on mic, looking at photo*) What are you talking about? This is a handlebar moustache. It's a classic gentleman's moustache.

> SOUND:
> AUDIO CLIP *continues.*

HANA: (*recorded*) Maybe that's the look you're going for, but as an Asian it looks like you have two question marks on your face.

RIÉ: Questionable look, questionable character.

> PROJECTION *out.*

When my sisters say stuff like that, deep down, I know they're probably right. They're always staging these interventions on me, half-joking, half-serious. But secretly I was just happy not to have to talk about my father's condition. They'd see for themselves soon enough.

When we got to my dad's hospital room, without a word my sisters dropped their coats and their bags and they climbed into bed with my dad. That blew my mind. They could've levitated and I would've been less impressed.

But they lay in bed with him. And they touched him the way daughters touch their fathers when there's a lot of love. All these hours I'd been spending with my dad: bringing him heated blankets, feeding him chips of ice, describing the weather outside his window, I can honestly say it never occurred to me to climb into his bed, to lie next to him, to touch him.

In the manner in which we express affection towards our father, my brother and I are like characters trapped in a Frank Capra movie. My brother Ken is a pastor and his favourite film is *It's a Wonderful Life*, and together we are about as fulsome in our expressions of affection as Jimmy Stewart. "Gee, Pa, just try and hang in there, will ya? And hand to God, you'll be as right as rain." Our brotherly affection is in black and white, but my sisters' love is in Technicolor, and in surround sound.

My sisters are multilingual in the languages of love. They coo, and cluck, and purr with mellifluous felicity. They speak in tongues, not because the Spirit has descended upon them, but because it never left.

Make no mistake, my sisters are grown women, mothers but not matronly, but maybe magicians, maybe wiccans, because in the blink of an eye they become little girls again. "Goodnight, Daddy, *otosan*, I love you, *ai shiteru*," cooing affectionate little girls, while my brother and I remain like British Beefeaters, arms by our sides, silent, while my sisters shapeshift into a basket full of kittens, and with every kiss they bring him back from the brink of death, and if this isn't magic, then I don't know what is.

And as I stand there, slack-jawed and dumb, in the corner of the room, all I can think is there are cultures in this world that prize sons over daughters. I know because I come from one of them. So stupid.

PROJECTION:
STILL IMAGE of sisters (from left to right,
SETSU, HANA, and RIÉ) in hospital
with Mr. Shigematsu (AKIRA).

When my father's condition stabilized, my sisters had to go back to their regular lives. But let me tell you, their example was not lost on me. I mean I didn't want to do it right in front of them, but as soon as they were around the corner, I was on that bed. Right on the edge. And I leaned over, and I patted his knee like no one was watching.

≈

SOUND:
AUDIO CLIP of historical recording of the
Emperor of Japan's surrender speech.

A common memory that my father shares with many Japanese of his generation in Japan is hearing the Emperor's voice on the radio for the very first time, announcing Japan's defeat, Japan's surrender. So while everyone else is crying around him, my dad is secretly hopeful, because he's thinking, "Well now that the war is over, maybe my father will finally come home." My grandfather was a prisoner of war.

Now back then in my father's small hometown of Kagoshima, the only form of transportation left intact was the train system. So once a day the train would make a stop at their local station. And my father being just a kid, not knowing any better, would go down to the station to look for his dad.

TETSURO: Now, Dad, I'm not saying yours was a fool's errand, but you didn't know if your dad was alive or dead, so you go down to the train station on the off chance that he'll just show up, but you're doing this every day, you're twelve years old! How long can you keep this up? A week, a month?

AKIRA: Oh, not very long. Perhaps, just over a year.

TETSURO: Why did you stop?

AKIRA: There was only one person left on the platform that day, far too old to be my father, but I could see it was him.

TETSURO: Dad, did you run to him? Did you hug him? Did you say I love you?

AKIRA: No, of course not!

TETSURO: Dad, father and son, parent and child, you haven't seen each other for years. You didn't know if the other was alive or dead. Are you telling me the moment you two saw each other there wasn't a single expression of relief, affection, love?

Pause.

AKIRA: It must have been the late afternoon when we walked home from the station, because our shadows were so long on the road. And although I cannot be certain, I suppose had my father glanced at my shadow, he may have seen a slight hop in my step.

≈

My dad has been dying for two years now, and he's been dragging my mom down with him. Together they lived in a small apartment near Stanley Park. That was their physical address, but in reality my mom was living in a hole in the ground.

I could visit my mom during the middle of a sunny day in their bright West End apartment, but with my father dying in what used to be their living room, the darkness was all around. I could dwell in that darkness with her, keep her company, but for all my jokes, I was just a tea candle, not enough to change anything.

My kids are special in the way that all kids are special. They don't have to do anything, they can just be. My mom could be trapped in a room that stinks with the stench of death, and I could carry in my sleeping child and their presence alone would banish all shadows.

I haven't told you about my wife because that story would take all day, all night. But if there's one thing I could share to help you understand who she is, it'd be this. One day, she said to me, "I think we should try and find a bigger place to rent, so your parents can live with us."

No, no, no, no! I like to walk around the house naked. How is that going to work? I just can't sit beside my father on the couch wearing nothing. Because even though he claims to be blind, I just know he'll turn in my direction and say something like –

AKIRA: Is it laundry day?

Or if he's feeling more sassy –

AKIRA: Are you going to audition for *Oh! Calcutta*?

Moving in together? That's a terrible idea. But once again, I was wrong. So now my little family lives with my parents under one roof. It's not perfect, but it's better. Especially for my mom. So now Grandma gets woken up early by the chaos of my kids getting ready for school, and she's kept up late by the bickering of my kids as they fight over the family iPad. And together this cacophony is more life-giving than springtime and birdsong. Every day my kids hug Grandma good morning and good night. My mom can survive anything, but no one should live without being touched.

≈

The only exercise my father got during his final days was walking to the bathroom. "Come on, Dad! If you walk any slower, you'll be standing still!" I walk behind him, watch his knees, and when they begin to wobble, I'll pop my head in where his love handles used to be, and say, "Put your arms around me, Dad." And he does.

With soft, cool hands, he'll clasp my neck, and I lift. Just over a hundred pounds. The weight of a supermodel really. Now, if I were walking past a modelling agency that was on fire, am I the kind of man who could save the day? Well, yes I am, yes I am.

And as I carry my father, I think about the terrible beauty of life. I have reached the peak of my physical powers during the very season my father has begun to fall.

My father is like a baby now. Colicky, so colicky, up-all-night colicky. He doesn't cry. This is my father after all. But he has these spells which the doctors never did figure out. So in Japanese, we just called it *kurushii*, agony. *Tasukete! Tasukete!* Help me. Help me. During these spells, which could last up to eleven hours, his blind eyes would blaze, and all the strength he lost through atrophy returned with a fury. He would grab the bed rails on both sides, and he shook the room.

During these spells, there was only one way to calm him down: rubbing his back, which was kind of hard to do over the railings, so I crawled into bed with my dad. It's actually kind of nice. I mean how often does a man get to experience physical intimacy with another man without it getting... intimate? So there I am, spooning my father, rubbing his back, when his buttocks begin to rhythmically bump up against my groin. It's the Parkinson's. He can't help it. But oh God, so awkward, so weird. This is the worst! But if this is the worst, then here it is. Soon enough I'm not even thinking about my dad's buttocks, I'm thinking about my arms. Marathon massages make your muscles ache. I can feel the lactic acid building up. I look down at my arms. I am the captain of the SS *Tetsuro*. Carry me. Carry me home. Carry me all the way to the end.

≈

My father was carried from our home for the last time on September 19, 2015. His instructions were to have his body donated to science; specifically, the Department of Cellular and Physiological Science at UBC. So for years I've been waiting for this white van to pull up, and then having to deal with a pair of movers as they manhandle my dad's dead body. But that's not what happened. The doorbell rang and there was a man with all the earnest sincerity of a young Mormon missionary. So I asked him –

TETSURO: How long have you been doing this job?

UNDERTAKER: Four months.

TETSURO: What do you know now that you didn't know before?

UNDERTAKER: Nothing. I mean we all know we're going to die, right? But I will say this – I do appreciate the littler things.

TETSURO: Like what?

By this time we were outside.

UNDERTAKER: Like the rain. Just being able to feel it on my skin because – these bodies I carry out – can't.

≈

SOUND:
AUDIO CLIP *of the plucking of a stringed instrument like the pinprick of rain.*

(*above*) Of all our family photos, in this one my father shows an uncharacteristic level of pride.

(*below*) My father is forty-three years old in this photo. I am forty-four.

*TETSURO changes his shirt and puts on his
jacket and a black tie during the following.*

Seventy-two percent. That's how much water is in your body. And
that water has been around here on earth for four and half billion
years. That means the moisture in your breath was once at the
centre of a glacier during the ice age. In your frozen form, you
carved valleys through unnamed mountain ranges.

And as many an ancient text will attest, there was once a Great
Flood. You rained for forty days and forty nights, until the whole
earth turned blue.

And on another day, a few years before you were born, you
were a cloud. And a young girl studied your ever-changing face,
wondering, "What will my children look like?"

And on another day, in complete darkness, you were an amniotic
sea, the temperature of blood, vibrating to the rhythm of two
heartbeats.

And one day, the water that is you, will not be you. But if you were
loved, maybe you will be the tears of someone who weeps for you.
Not because they're crying, but because they're laughing so hard at
the memory of how pathetic you looked, that time you got caught
in the rain. And as they dab their cheeks, they'll stop to wonder,
are you in heaven? When in fact you have never been so near.

> *PROJECTION:*
> *STILL IMAGE of AKIRA outside the
> BBC External Services offices in London.
> TETSURO turns to look at him.*

END OF PLAY

Acknowledgments

TO DONNA, for giving my dad A Room to Die In, for giving my family a place to live, and for giving me a reason to rise at four every morning to fight the good fight.

TO RICHARD, for being the first theatre person in this town to take a chance on me. May we have many more collaborations to come.

TO HEIDI, in the heat of creative battle as you keep the forces of chaos and confusion at bay, the twin blades of your incisive questions and conceptual rigour are so sharp, I can shed my trusty armour because I know you will always have my back.

TO HEATHER, for having the courage to bet on our little company and all the big things for which we stand. Your faith inspires us.

TO GERALD, the flock is happy because you take such good care of the shepherd. What a privilege it is to stand in the light of your genius.

TO BONNIE, for your time and for your friendship. Your belief in us sustains our belief in ourselves.

TO WENDY, you have always been VACT's First Friend and our most loyal ally. We strive to be worthy of the trust you have placed in us.

TO ANDREA, before I interviewed my father, you interviewed me, and your stirring descriptions of that which was not yet written remain the heights to which *Empire* continues to aspire.

TO TIFF, for showing me that those inspiring late-night, mind-expanding conversations didn't end with my art-school adolescence.

TO BELLE, new ideas are so delicate. They can be killed by a frown or a smirk. When *Empire* was at its most vulnerable, your vote of confidence was all the affirmation it needed to survive.

TO ANNIE, the least-fake person I know. The sincerity of your smiles, nods, and laughter is the only compass I need to find my way.

TO YVONNE, for being the first person to trust me with a microphone and for your continued recklessness in remaining my co-conspirator.

TO LAARA, of all the extravagant treasures that have come into my life thanks to our mutual friend, your friendship is the one I treasure most.

TO INS, for inspiring me not to be just a better artist, but a better person. Thank you for being our community's Neil Armstrong.

TO JANET, when a stranger handed you *Rising Son* on VHS, you responded by inviting me to your wedding. Your embrace gave me my first sense of belonging, and I have felt at home in the world ever since.

TO ANN-MARIE, for the honour of recognition as a writer-in-residence at Historic Joy Kogawa House, for serving as my trusted editor with a jeweller's eye. Before an artist can flourish, they need someone like you in their life. I bask in your warmth and your light.

TO KEVIN, it would have made my father proud to see me published. Thank you for making his dream a reality.

TO JERRY, for opening doors for me where I saw only walls. Before I had ever conceived of publication, you offered to buy copies of my script to teach to your classes long before opening night. How could I ever repay such confidence in my work?

TO JOSEPH, for always upping my game. I was unduly proud of my grantsmanship until I met you. I remain your biggest fan.

TO JANE and ROSS, for your encouragement, your ardent support, your insightful feedback, and your revivifying warmth.

TO ALLAN, my first mentor. Had you been anything less than magnificent, I would have become a lawyer.

TO HOWARD, for being such a role model of possibility. Your abundant generosity with your wisdom stokes our ambition.

TO THERESA, for teaching me that Italian dads can also be incapable of expressing their feelings, for attending my father's memorial, and for raising the flag on *Empire* so high the whole world could see. You are a true friend.

TO SHELDON and KURT, the spectacle that is *Empire* was built upon a cornerstone made possible by your kindness and generosity.

TO ANNALIES, The Cultch is my artistic home, and all that began when you extended your friendship to me even when I was just another theatregoer in the lobby.

TO JESSA, for your fulsome understanding of my work. It has always made me feel seen.

TO SHELLEY, for always being there when I need you, and I always will.

TO KG, forgive the analogy but you were the prom queen everyone loved, and I was the new transfer student nobody liked. But with every intro (and extro), you made it clear to everyone that you were proud of my antics, and eventually the others came around. I wouldn't have lasted without you.

TO HEATHER K, for plucking me from obscurity and taking a chance on me. I still use the lessons you taught me.

TO BILL, for always being so kind, so complimentary, and so generous. I never stopped being star-struck around you. It was an honour to sit in your chair.

o Shigematsu

re than twenty years, Tetsuro Shigematsu has been telling
across an array of media. He is a writer, actor, performance
roadcaster, stand-up comic, scholar, filmmaker, and theatre
Originally trained in the fine arts, he found a similar creative
riting for CBC Television's *This Hour Has 22 Minutes.* Then
he became the first person-of-colour to host a daily national
gram in Canada when he took over *The Roundup* on CBC
here he co-wrote and co-produced nearly a thousand hours
rk programming. He has written and produced more than
es of radio drama as well as the feature film *Yellow Fellas*
He is currently a Vanier scholar and PhD candidate at the
y of British Columbia.

reator conversant across a wide variety of media, Tetsuro
examining the subject matter and asking what form the
s to take. Rather than forcing narratives into the traditional
s of that medium, he often innovates new aesthetic forms
ss with greater fidelity the contours of lived experience.
g pieces are often singular and groundbreaking. His most
atre work, *Empire of the Son,* sold out its run before it
d was named the best show of 2015 by the *Vancouver Sun*
g remounted at The Cultch in 2016. It has been produced
da, including the National Arts Centre in Ottawa, Centaur
ontreal, Factory Theatre in Toronto, Festival Players of
ard County in Ontario, Artistic Fraud of Newfoundland,
United States through the National Asian American The-
tion Festival in Ashland, Oregon.

award-winning body of work in film, television, radio,
and theatre continues to be taught in Canadian and
iversities as examples of creative possibility.
m @tweetsuro or visit him at shiggy.com.

TO JOEL AND DEBORAH, for tending the brightest fire in the
city, and letting me join the warm glow of your circle.

TO MY PHD COMMITTEE, TERESA, CARL, RITA, and
GEORGE, thank you for dissuading me from embarking on a
more orthodox thesis and instead guiding me towards the mountain passes of *Empire of the Son*. It is your wisdom "that has made
all the difference."

TO MARIE FRANCE, for your fiery intellect and inspiring words.
You gave me the courage I needed to leap into the unknown.

TO DANIEL and DAVE, for the game plan and the pep talk. We
wouldn't have had the audacity if you hadn't given us the time.

TO JOYCE and TOM, for approaching me way back when, and
inviting me to join the cause. Thank you for giving my life purpose.

TO RAY and TERRY, for being VACT's most loyal artists. Thank
you for putting up with me throughout all these years.

TO JAYSON, for being such a badass rock and roller. I want to
steal your magical camper truck with you in it.

TO FLO, your style and effervescent personality always make
even the shadow side seem glamorous.

TO REMY, I'll be glad of the day when someone replaces me in
Empire, if only so I can finally see these wonders.

TO CAROLE, your ingenious ability to make real the notions I
could only muse on thrilled me to no end.

TO BARBARA, from *Salmon Row* to *Empire of the Son*, you
always make me look and feel like a leading man.

TO STEVE, for giving me the best scene partner a solo performer
could ever have. Your music provokes me, moves me, inspires me,
yet never stands in my light.

TO JAMIE, for inspiring me to one day have conversations with Mika not just as father and daughter but as colleagues. You're the coolest young person I know. Please hire me one day when you become Queen of Everything.

TO MARIA, thank you for risking life and limb before each show to assist with my unconventional vocal warm-ups.

TO PAM, for beginning a dialogue with the audience before I even emerge from your spectacular set.

TO SUSAN, for being my *oneesan* (even though I'm older than you). When my father died and it felt like the work was about to derail, the fullness of your acceptance and the depth of your solidarity kept me grounded.

TO LAURA, for reminding me that the reflected light of the moon is always more beautiful than the incandescence of the sun.

TO KALSANG, ARANKA, DAN, and ZARAH. For these past couple of years, my life has become so narrowly monastic. Being able to occasionally spend time with such an attractive, loyal group of friends has allowed me to maintain this pleasant fiction of having a well-rounded life. May our children intermarry so we can remain family for always.

TO MAS, for all that you've done, for all that is to come. This next one is for you.

TO RIÉ, for leaving your own family to spend one hundred and one days to be by Dad's side.

TO SETSU, for rescuing Dad from the hospital so he could die at home. Thank you for Japan.

TO HANA, for being Dad's favourite (and everyone else's, including me), and for always being so kind.

TO KEN, for inspiring me to be a better father.

TO MIKA, for allowing me to include
forward to your maturation as an a
your ideas. You have the sweet gentle
affection of Mommy, and even more

TO TAIZO, I hope one day you wil
my show. And may such forgivene
own one-man show about your
humiliated you before hundreds o
it using a Jewish Brooklyn accent,
giggling with childlike joy.

TO MOM, living with you has b
grant Dad the patience he will n

TO DAD, for being the kind of r
person she has ever met. I don't
but it is always good to feel you

TO THE PERSON I will neve
ence, you listened with such lu
performance shifted into auto
logue: Who are you? What ar
story? Even though I will nev
tions, I take solace in knowin
eyes of a stranger. For me, thi
powerful than movies. You v
between us except the air
we held like smooth pebble

TO BAHAREH, my empre
I have ever known.